The Church in the Valley

Flaunden Old Church

The Church in the Valley

Flaunden Old Church

T. J. Leary

Outside cover illustrations: plates from the book and a detail from the East Window in Flaunden New Church (front) and the site of the old church today (back)

Title page: Flaunden Old Church from the north west. Coloured engraving by W.B. Cooke (1778-1855) of the painting by Henry Munro *c.* 1815
MacLeod Matthews Collection

Contents

List of Illustrations and Maps

Foreword

Preface

1   Settlement in the Chess Valley   1

2   Flaunden Old Church   4

3   Furnishings   10

4   Memorials   23

5   Flaunden Church today   30

Appendix 1. Photographs of Flaunden Old Church in the Hertfordshire Archives   35

Appendix 2. Papal Bull regarding burials at Flaunden Old Church   35

Appendix 3. Extracts from the will of Richard Prince   37

Appendix 4. Petition submitted for the Consecration of Flaunden New Church   38

Bibliography and Abbreviations   39

Index of Names   42

General Index   44

Illustrations and Maps

Plan of St Mary Magdalene, Flaunden – *inside front cover*

Map 1   Detail from OS 6-inch England & Wales Hertfordshire Sheet XXXVIII.SW 1899 showing Flaunden and Latimer – *inside back cover*

2   Detail from the 1968 'Seventh Series' OS map showing Flaunden and Latimer – *inside back cover*

Plate 1   The Chess Valley today from the west

2   Latimer Park Farm today

3   Delivering water to the new Flaunden Village *c.* 1910

4   Engraving of the Munro painting (see title page)

5   Plan of Flaunden Old Church and adjoining Priest's House

6   View of Flaunden Old Church from the north west

7   View of Flaunden Old Church from the south east

8   The West door in 1906

9   Service to mark the Festival of St Mary Magdalene, 22 July 1928

10   Wall painting in the north transept

11   Replacement bell at St John's, Uxbridge Moor today

12   The Flaunden bell, showing the date and William Knight's initials

13   Inscription on the bell

14   The old clapper from the bell

15   Chalice and paten

16   Salver given by Richard Prince

17   Drawing of the font in Flaunden Old Church

18   The font today

19   Nineteenth-century watercolour of the tiles now in Flaunden New Church

20   Off-centred tile stamp

21   Traces of the bust of a crowned king on one of the medieval tiles

22   Forward-facing lion

23   Pierced saltire tile

24   Communion rail

25   The South door

26   Mass Dial

27   An incomplete consecration cross?

28   Extract from the notebook in the Latimer Church Archives

29   Detail from the marble slab in the Latimer Vestry

30   Blore's plan for Latimer Church

31   The clock in Flaunden New Church

32   Drawing by Herbert Edmunds in 1910, showing Richard Prince's tomb

33 & 34   Railings from Richard Prince's tomb

35   Arms of the Prince Family?

36   William Liberty's tomb

37   One of the corner markers from William Liberty's tomb

38   Inscription on William Liberty's tomb

39   The Grimsdell tomb

40   Flaunden New Church

41   The old Baptist Chapel in Flaunden

42   Note from Lady Susan Trueman about Gilbert Scott and Flaunden New Church

43   The Revd Samuel King

44   Sir Gilbert Scott

45   Dedication Board in Flaunden New Church

Foreword

Visitors to Flaunden may have noticed, when passing the church of St Mary Magdalene on the way down to Latimer, a track leading off to the left near a sign reading 'Old Church Lane'. Most will have thought no further, but some may have paused and wondered how the name came about. In this detailed and yet very readable and generously illustrated book, Tim Leary has given us the answer, describing the early settlement of the Chess Valley, the establishment there of a medieval village and the building of the first Flaunden church on the banks of the river in about 1235.

My family has owned the land surrounding the church for many years but, although we knew it was there, we knew very little about it. Indeed, given that it is now just a pile of stones covered in nettles and we have been taken up with more immediate concerns, we have had little incentive to explore either it or, indeed, the site of the neighbouring village.

As Tim explains, however, the church was of considerable architectural interest. He describes its original design and subsequent extension before turning to its decoration and furnishing. He recounts stories of the services held there, once a month and weather permitting since the curate had to come from Hemel Hempstead. He also speaks of those buried there, and in particular members of the Prince family, its principal benefactors. Finally, he discusses the reasons for its abandonment in 1838 when the present church was built on a much more convenient site in the current village; and he charts the sorry dilapidation of the old church.

All this has been a revelation to me personally but, as well as documenting an important part of our local history, Tim's work will be of similar interest to the current members of the Flaunden congregation and community, especially as many of the furnishings of the old church were transferred to the new.

It will also appeal to those walking along the Chess Valley or visiting neighbouring Latimer, whose own church has long been served by the same clergy. Perhaps it will inspire renewed interest in preserving the old Flaunden church!

Charles MacLeod Matthews
Chenies Manor

Preface

This brief history of Flaunden Old Church is intended as a companion and even complement to my history of St Mary Magdalene, Latimer (see the bibliography). Inevitably, it repeats some of the information in the earlier book, but I hope not more than is necessary for a fluent and comprehensible narrative. It contains much of relevance to the 'new' church at Flaunden as well as some to Latimer, and should therefore be of interest to local residents; but my hope is that it will also interest visitors to the area, whether staying at Latimer House or following the Chess Valley walk. Those who want to pursue matters in greater detail can begin by consulting some of the scholarly works listed in the bibliography, to which all further references relate.

Several attempts, most notably by the Revd H.E. Fitzherbert in the late 1920s, but also more recently, have been made to inspire interest in and conserve the remains of the old church. However, as was noted in 1976, 'Time, decay and vandalism have triumphed. Today there is nothing left but ridges of rubble marking the plan of the church and broken masonry scattered among the trees' (Bastin 27). At the time of writing, there are little more than heaps of stone, covered by undergrowth (see the back cover). It is my hope nevertheless that, by drawing attention to it and the artefacts now in the new church, this book will help in inspiring revived efforts to preserve what is an important part of local history, and of church and architectural history in general.

Unless considered of particular relevance, specific references are given only for direct quotations. Otherwise, the principal sources are listed at the end of every chapter.

All photographs were taken by me, unless indicated otherwise in the image captions; all other images are in the public domain, have been made available by the owner and/or the copyright holder (acknowledged in the image captions), or are no longer subject to copyright restrictions. Similarly, unless otherwise stated, all transcriptions and translations are mine.

Acknowledgement is due to the following for help in various ways with this book: Dr David Ashby, Joe Barclay, Mike Brace, Shaun Burgin, Mrs Elizabeth Chalmers (Church Recording Society), Dr Trevor Chalmers, Chris Cockle, Paul Drury FSA, Michael Farley FSA, Dr Meryl Foster OBE, Mrs Sophie Hammond and the Oxford DAC, Sam Hatfield (Chiltern Open Air Museum), Paul Jennings, Ben

Jones, Dr Helen Leary (Churchwarden, St Mary Magdalene, Latimer), the Revd Dr Brian Ludlow, Colin Mantripp, Michael Mason, Roderick McCulloch, Dr Wendy Morrison FSA, Dr Bridget Nichols, Mrs Andrea Norman (Churchwarden, St Mary Magdalene, Flaunden), Michael Palmer, Dr Mark Philpott, Neil Rees, Stephen Rickerby, the Revd Dr Stephen Roberts, Mrs Helen Savage (Churchwarden, St Mary Magdalene, Flaunden), Lisa Shekede, David Taylor, Michael Todd KC, Dr Tony Trowles FSA, Professor Michael Winterbottom FBA, and the Very Revd John Witcombe. Also, the librarians and archivists of the Bodleian Library in Oxford, the British Library, the Buckinghamshire Archives, Hertfordshire Archives and Local Studies, the Hillingdon Local Studies, Archives and Museum Service, and the Lincolnshire Archives. Of course, although they have improved my work greatly, they bear no responsibility for any flaws that remain.

T.J. Leary
Chorleywood, March 2024

Chapter 1. Settlement in the Chess Valley

The ruins of Flaunden Old Church, dedicated to St Mary Magdalene, lie on the north bank of the River Chess, between Latimer and Chenies, and are easily viewed by those taking a short detour from the Chess Valley Walk. The medieval village lay immediately to the west. It was a 'cluster' village, that is one which was not built around a central village green, and nothing of it remains standing today, although, in certain light, outlines can be seen on the ground. A survey of soil marks and debris made after ploughing work in 1966 suggested that it covered an area of about 250 by 700 feet (about 75 by 200 metres), and this is supported by the 2018-19 Chilterns AONB LiDAR (Light Detection and Ranging) project. The flint trackway, which crosses the site and is now used by farm vehicles, preserves the route of a very early thoroughfare. (See Map 1 and Plate 1.)

Plate 1. The Chess Valley today from the west showing the sites of the church and village. Note the width of the valley at this point.

The Chess Valley is post-glacial and was probably formed by melt-water. It is therefore much wider than might be expected from the size of the relatively youthful chalk stream which flows down it, and flat areas with a ready supply of water and flint were conducive to settlement from the earliest times. The valleys also ensured ease of travel and communication, since the slopes on either side were probably wooded.

Roman settlements have been identified at Sarratt, Chenies and Chesham, and the nearby Latimer, at what is now Latimer Park Farm. (See Map 2 and Plate 2.) This settlement was abandoned in the mid-fourth century, to be replaced a little later by a timber construction occupied by huntsmen and small farmers. The site was abandoned once more in the sixth century, after which the area reverted to scrub and wasteland.

Plate 2. Latimer Park Farm today, from Latimer House.
Again, note the width of the Chess Valley.

The Chess Valley was not settled again until the establishment of Chesham (*Ceastelhamm*) by the Middle Saxons, attracted again by the supply of water and, in particular, chalybeate or iron-bearing springs. The Medieval period then saw the appearance of a number of dispersed hamlets, separated by woodland. As before, river valleys constituted the main routes of travel and communication.

One of these hamlets was, of course, Flaunden, probably established around the first millennium. It is not mentioned in the Domesday Book (completed in 1086) since it was then part of the Manor of Hemel Hempstead. (Indeed, it may have been from Hemel Hempstead that the earliest inhabitants of Flaunden came.) In the 1200s, a Manor of Flaunden was held as a separate entity by one Nicholas de Flaunden, and then by his son Thomas, but the manorial rights seem to have reverted to Hemel Hempstead by the 1540s.

The site of the village, from which Nicholas de Flaunden would have drawn his name, is possibly reflected by the word 'Flaunden': -*den* probably derives from *denu*, the Old English for a valley (hence the title of this book), while *Flaun-* may come from the Old English *flage* or 'slab': the hamlet was built on a solid platform in a marshy valley. Ironically, while proximity to water might have been one of the reasons for settling on the site (ready water-supply aside, there may also have been a nearby ford across the Chess), and flooding might have been one of the reasons for abandoning the village and moving up the hill (see Chapter 5), the new village was sometimes beset by water-supply failures, when water had to be brought in by cart from Latimer (Plate 3).

Plate 3: Delivering water to the new Flaunden Village c. 1910,
perhaps during the great heatwave and drought of 1911
Latimer Village Box

Flaunden Old Church was built by Thomas de Flaunden by 1235 'in the Vale near the River, for the Ease of himself and the Conveniency of his Tenants' (Chauncy 476), the parish church of St Mary's, Hemel Hempstead being at some distance. (The date is fixed by the appointment in 1235 of Bernardus de Graveleigh to the Vicarage of Hemel Hempstead with the chapels of Flaunden and Bovingdon, in the Diocese of Lincoln and the Deanery of Berkhamsted.) An indication of its significance is that the site of the village is marked as 'Maudlaine' in the earliest county map of Hertfordshire, by Christopher Saxton in 1577.

The village has not been excavated, but surface finds include 'some two to three dozen sherds of 13th-14th century date, from both glazed and unglazed vessels' (Branigan 1968, 400).

Sources: Bastin, Beresford, Branigan 1968, Branigan 1971, Chauncy, Cussans, Ekwall, Farley 2000, Farley 2010, *HCH* II, LiDAR, Mawer, Notebook

Chapter 2. Flaunden Old Church

Plate 4. Engraving of the Munro painting by W.B. Cooke (see title page), showing the
additions to the west of the original design
Flaunden Church Collection

Although now a neglected ruin, Flaunden Old Church is a Scheduled Monument (BU 151), with Grade II listing, and is, or was, of considerable architectural interest, having originally been built in the shape of a Greek cross (see inside front cover), a testimony to the building's early date. There are only three other churches in Hertfordshire built on this plan, at Sarratt and Letchworth, although both were altered later, and Buntingford, although originally just a nave and chancel.

As befits a village or hamlet with a small population (just 44 conformists and 23 nonconformists are recorded in the 1676 Compton Census), and although later expanded, the building was initially small, measuring internally just 36 feet from east to west and 37 feet from north to south, across the transepts. The nave and chancel were only 13 feet wide. There was a doorway at the west end of the nave, dating to the building's first construction, which is depicted in the Edmunds drawing of 1910 (see Plates 8 and 32). There was a further doorway in the north wall of the chancel, where there had originally been just a recess and there was a window on the south side. The east window can be seen in Plate 7. The south transept, just ten and a half feet wide, contained a partly restored three-light window dating to the fifteenth century (see Plate 9). The correspondingly narrow north transept had, in contrast, just a single-light window.

While the church was small inside, the walls were very thick, measuring two and a half feet, making the building look much larger than it was. They were made of flint rubble with clunch, that is limestone dressing, built on foundations which included blocks of pudding stone.

Built on the west end was a square wooden belfry, possibly topped by small spike (the 'Hertfordshire Spike'). This must pre-date the Edwardian Inventory of 1552, which speaks of bells in the steeple (see Chapter 3). Later, accommodation for the priest was built on to the west of the church. This was colonised later still by poor families. The plan inside the front cover is to be compared with that drawn in 1824 by J. Buckler, and his views of the church (Plates 5 and 7, cf. 4 and 6.) The priest's accommodation is not shown in the 1898 (2nd ed.) OS map (see the bibliography and Map 1), and had presumably fallen down by the time the map was surveyed.

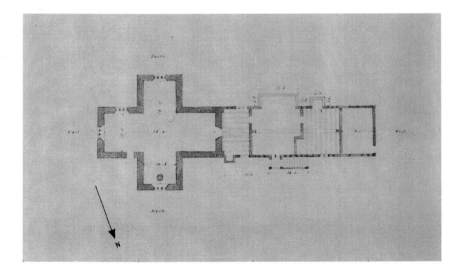

Plate 5. Plan of Flaunden Old Church and adjoining Priest's House, J. Buckler 1824
Flaunden Church Collection

*Plate 6. View of Flaunden Old Church from the north west
by 'A Subscriber',* The Builder, *23 March 1844*

Plate 7. View of Flaunden Old Church from the south east, J. Buckler 1824
Flaunden Church Collection

As is shown by Plates 4 and 6-7, the church building, including its later extensions, was in reasonable shape not long before Flaunden New Church was built in 1838 (see Chapter 5); but it had deteriorated greatly by the time it was described in *HCH* II in 1908: by then, the east wall of the chancel had collapsed although parts of the north and south walls remained, as did the walls and gables of both transepts and the nave, although they were entirely unroofed. On the east wall of the south transept, there were traces of a stone reredos with a central niche over it. A small thirteenth-century piscina was set in the south wall. (Compare Appendix 1.) For the west door, see Plate 8.

Plate 8. The West door in 1906
© Hertfordshire Archives and Local Studies DE/X1042/8/14a

Twenty years later, enough of the south transept was still standing to provide the backdrop for the patronal service (see Plate 9); but attempts made then to raise interest in the building and its preservation did not bear fruit and, with the roof gone, further dilapidation was rapid. This was hastened by the predations of those after building material for rockeries and the like (cf. Plate 42), resulting in what can be seen today (see the back cover).

Plate 9. Service to mark the Festival of St Mary Magdalene, 22 July 1928
View from of the south transept
Flaunden Church Collection

The Edwardian Inventory (see Chapter 3) mentions 'an old vestment for worke days,' which might suggest that in 1552 and, no doubt before, services were held during the week as well as on Sundays; but this was certainly not the case later. Services were conducted just one Sunday afternoon a month, taken by a curate sent by the Vicar of Hemel Hempstead, and conducted only when the weather was fine; sometimes there was an interval between services of several months. Cussans (180) tells of a labourer who reported that he had often known corpses to remain up to five days in the church, once they had become too malodorous to be kept in people's houses, until a clergyman came for a burial service. He observes, further, that, being in an almost forgotten part of the Diocese of Lincoln, Flaunden was neglected by the clergy. This might account for the large number of Dissenters in the area (see Chapter 4).

Clerical neglect of Flaunden may not have been entirely wilful, however, at any rate at local level, where staffing difficulties and financial considerations were always a considerable factor: Bovingdon and Flaunden had a curate each in 1656, but the Revd William Bingham, who died in 1819, was not only the Vicar of Hemel Hempstead but also of Great Gaddesden, the perpetual curate of

Bovingdon and Flaunden and the minister of the Quebec Chapel in London. Since he had just one assistant curate, it is not surprising that services at Flaunden Old Church were irregular.

Apparently, on fine days when a service was due, a watchman was stationed in Bovingdon Church tower to watch the Hemel Hempstead road and ring the bell to summon the parishioners if he saw the parson coming. Another of the stories concerning services at Flaunden Old Church is reported, with some reservations, by Cussans (179) in a footnote:

> I have some hesitation in recording the following story, inasmuch as I have heard it applied to another parish, but I give it on the authority of a gentleman living in the neighbourhood, who is old enough to have remembered the incident, if it really occurred here. A party of ladies and gentlemen, who were on a visit to Lord Chesham, at Latimers, walked down to old Flaunden church. [Presumably the first or, possibly, the second Lord Chesham is meant.] At that time there were three or four families, not living exactly in the church, but under the roof of the church, which had been extended so as to cover their cottages, built against its walls. "How very interesting," remarked one of the party, "I should so like to attend service here." "Well, to-morrow is the regular day," replied the woman who was showing them over the church, "but I do hope and trust it will rain, and then the parson won't come, for I've got one of my best hens a sitting on thirteen eggs in the pulpit, and she won't come off till Tuesday".

In other versions, the bird concerned is a goose and according to Bastin, 26, 'The curate completed the formalities of [his] visit by recording in the registers that "Parson Goose" had occupied the pulpit on this occasion.'

Sources: Bastin, Branigan 1968, British Listed Buildings, *Buckinghamshire Examiner*, Chauncy, Clutterbuck, Cussans, Flaunden Church Archives, *HCH* II, Heritage Portal, *IHM*, Lawrence et al., 1898 OS map, Pemberton, Pevsner, Salmon, Whiteman

Chapter 3. Furnishings

Commissioners were appointed in 1552, under Edward VI, to make an inventory of 'goodes, plate, juells, vestyments, bells and other ornyments within every paryshe belonging or in any wyse apperteying to any churche, chapell, brotherhed, gylde or fraternytye within this our realme of Englond' (The National Archives catalogue description, E117). The declared intention behind this inventory was to stop private embezzlement of church goods after the dissolution of the monasteries, although, the following year, a further commission was directed to seize church goods to supplement the royal coffers. It was also intended to remove from churches anything redolent of Catholicism. Whatever its purpose, however, it is a useful source of information for the historian.

The inventory for the old church at Flaunden (The National Archives E 315/497) is quoted in full by Cussans (178) and lists *inter alia* altar cloths and vestments, a 'Lattyn' (i.e. brass) cross, candlesticks and censer, and two handbells. The church was therefore well supplied, and many of its furnishings made their way to the new church in 1838. It is to these that this chapter is principally devoted.

Not all the church furnishings and decoration have survived, although the piscina and reredos in the south transept could still be seen in 1910 (cf. Chapter 2). So could traces of wall painting, a painting in the north transept 'probably representing the crucifixion' (*IHM* II). In fact the painting shows an angel lit by projecting rays to the left (see Plate 10) and the figure might have been part of an Annunciation scene, with the Virgin Mary possibly depicted on the opposite window splay. Earlier, Salmon (118) reported, in the 'East Chancel' window, 'a large defaced Figure, which has been fine.' Near it is an 'obscure writing', which he transcribes as *Auctor qui istam fenestram fecerant*. Presumably, there was something before *auctor*, to account for the plural verb: '[The ... and] designer who had built this window'.

Although he does not give his source, the author of the Notebook in the Latimer Church Archives (see bibliography) is worth quoting (his contractions are tacitly expanded): 'The three remaining windows are perpendicular. That in the North Transept is of carved oak ... Some of the commandments were painted in an old character on the South wall ... In the South Transept was an altar and a niche above it, in the East wall, and a piscina in the South wall. Four sockets (for candles) remain in the stone ... The lower part of the niche is painted nearly of a black colour: In the upper part, on a ground of dark scroll work, is a dove with expanded wings, apparently the remains of a nimbus round the head. This wall has been painted at one time in a diaper pattern of pale blue squares, separated with white bands, edged by black lines. At another date it appears to have been nearly all of a red colour. Near the South window, and in other parts of the Chancel, there are crosses contained in a nimbus, painted in red [Rough sketch: four circles contained by a larger circle] … In the side of the window in the North Transept there is the figure of an angel painted in Indian red.' (Compare the quotation from *IHM* II above.)

Plate 10. The angel wall painting in the north transept
© *Hertfordshire Archives and Local Studies DE/X1042/8/15b*

As well as listing handbells, the Edwardian Inventory lists 'Imprimis thre Belles in the Steple'. There were three bells in the tower, when the old church was abandoned in 1838, one of which has long been lost. Of the remaining two, one (a treble bell) was installed in Flaunden New Church, and the other was hung in the newly built St John's Church, Uxbridge Moor. This church was deconsecrated in 1993 and is now a private house. The bell has been replaced by a later casting (see Plate 11). Despite exhaustive searches, the whereabouts of the original bell are now unknown. It is likely that the two lost bells were sold to help finance the building of the new church.

Plate 11. The replacement bell at St John's, Uxbridge Moor today

Both the Flaunden and St John's bells were inscribed with the date 1578 and the initials of the founder, William Knight, from a bell-casting dynasty in Reading (Plate 12). Although the earliest surviving examples of Knight's work, they therefore post-date the bells mentioned in the Inventory. It is, however, possible that the 1578 casting might have used metal from the earlier bells. There is no record of who funded the bells, but it is possible that the Prince family paid for them. (For the Prince family and their other benefactions, see below and Chapter 4.) Although there is no paperwork regarding the Flaunden bell, Knight charged 63 shillings and a penny for re-casting a bell of similar size at about the same time.

As a rule, Elizabethan bells (1559-84) bear no more than the founder's name and the date. The Flaunden and St John's bells are therefore unusual in having inscriptions, although their ungrammatical Latin is unsurprising. The Flaunden bell has a Maltese Cross and, in a black letter or Gothic script uncharacteristic of William Knight, *Gloria in exelcisc deo* or 'Glory to God in the highest' (Plate 13). The St John's bell also had a Maltese Cross and *sancta iohani ora pro nobis* ('Saint John, pray for us'), 'a very late instance of a distinctly pre-Reformation invocation' (North 35). Possibly, the reference to St John is why the bell was acquired for the church in Uxbridge Moor when it left Flaunden.

The Flaunden bell was renovated and rehung by the Whitechapel Foundry during work on the new church in 1987-8 and in 1990 the clapper was replaced. The old clapper, of wood and iron, is kept in the clock case in the Gallery (Plate 14).

Plate 12. The Flaunden bell, showing the date and William Knight's initials
Image courtesy of David Taylor

Plate 13. The inscription on the bell
Photographed from NADFAS

Plate 14. The old clapper from the bell

The Edwardian Inventory also includes 'It(e)m a Challic of Sillver p(ar)cell guilt poz xij oz', that is a silver chalice partially gilded and weighing 12 ounces. This is now lost: presumably it was melted down to supplement the Royal purse. The commissioners appointed to compile the inventory were instructed to list everything of precious metal, save the least valuable chalice and paten in the church; but these were soon discarded: under the new Protestant regulations, the whole congregation took wine at communion, and pre-reformation chalices, which held just enough wine for the priest, became inadequate. Also, it was realised that the only way to stop the secret celebration of the Roman Mass was to remove the remaining chalices. Between 1562 and 1576, each diocese was told to replace all chalices with communion cups.

Flaunden Old Church acquired a silver chalice or communion cup of a style typical of the 1560-70s, which, given its age, is in remarkable condition. Parish tradition records that it was donated by Queen Elizabeth I, who stayed several times at Chenies Manor, although this is undocumented. There is also a small cover paten made in 1576-7 and with 1577 engraved on its foot. These are now stored off-site, but can be used on special occasions (see Plate 15).

Plate 15. The chalice and paten

Another piece of silver from the old church is a rectangular salver inscribed in copperplate lettering *Donum Richardi Prince Gen: 1738*: 'The gift of Richard Prince Gen(tleman): 1738' (Plate 16). Its top surface is heavily scored, possibly by a knife used to cut communion bread.

Plate 16. The salver given by Richard Prince

A drawing survives of the font in the old church, before it was moved to the present one, with its original stem and base (Plate 17); the current base dates to the mid-nineteenth century (see Plate 18). With lead lining the octagonal bowl, and with quatrefoils set in a circle on each face, it is a fine example of perpendicular, medieval stonework. It dates to the thirteenth-fifteenth centuries, and possibly before the Papal Bull of 1477 (see Appendix 2), which confirms that Flaunden Old Church was accustomed to conduct all forms of divine service apart from burials - contrary to the historical practice for chapels of ease.

Plate 17. Drawing of font in Flaunden
Old Church by J. Buckler, 1842
Flaunden Church Collection

Plate 18. The font today

Also from the old church are the tiles now in the porch of the new. Those on either side are plain red, but the space between them is laid with patterned tiles which still bear traces of designs imprinted in white clay on a red base. They were already worn in 1910, however, and very little of the original glaze now remains.

What has been lost can be appreciated from Cussans (176-7), who says of them, 'Some are covered with arabesque patterns, and on others are lions, in various attitudes, and the heads of kings, queens and saints. On several appears the upper part of the figure of our Lord, in the act of benediction.' Cussans' comments can be supplemented in the light of subsequent work and knowledge, and also by reference to a nineteenth-century watercolour of some of the tiles, which is now in the Hertfordshire Archives, inserted in an unbound copy of Clutterbuck (see Plate 19).

Plate 19. Nineteenth-century watercolour of the tiles now in Flaunden New Church, annotated (with allowance for artistic licence) according to Christopher Hohler's tile-design classification

© Hertfordshire Archives and Local Studies DE/Cl/Z8/172 vol. 2 p.368

There is no record of where the tiles were in the old church, from where they were obtained or when they were laid; but they are of two sizes (6 inches and four and a half inches square) and seem to have been supplied in at least two stages during the fourteenth century. Three of the tiles depicted in Plate 19 (P12, P36 and P98) are standard later fourteenth-century designs from Penn, the most prominent of the Chiltern tileries. These are some of the smaller tiles on either side of the porch, although the stamp used for P36, which is off-centre, appears to have been designed for a slightly larger one. With the watercolour, compare Plate 20.

Plate 20. The off-centred tile stamp (P36)

The large tiles include the bust of a crowned king in a circular frame (Plates 19 and 21). This tile is similar in design to Hohler's P18 and matches one found at Beacon Hill in Penn, which, it has been suggested, 'is the forerunner of later known Penn forms' (Cauvain 47). It is therefore both rare and important evidence.

Plate 21. Traces of the bust of a crowned king on one of the medieval tiles

Also of note is the tile depicting a forward-facing lion with a mouth in a concave arc, since there appears to be just one parallel, in the Museum of London (A16883): see Plate 22. This too is probably a design of the formative, early phase of Penn production, although at Flaunden the stamp has been used on a smaller tile. Because it is at the side of the porch, it is relatively unworn. Also relatively unworn is the early phase tile depicted in Plate 23 (P88 or P89), several examples of which were laid in the floor.

Plate 22. The forward-facing lion   *Plate 23. Pierced saltire tile*

Wood from the old church was used for the Communion rail (Plate 24) and the south door. This, being machine made and therefore of Victorian rather than medieval manufacture, cannot itself have been brought from the old church (Plate 25). That said, the hinges on the door are riveted on and the slots in some of the screw heads are not central, so the metalwork looks pre-Victorian and might be seventeenth or eighteenth century. Perhaps this was brought across.

Plate 24. The Communion rail   *Plate 25. The South door*

So-called 'mass dials', which are found (generally on the south wall) in many medieval churches, are a primitive form of sundial. Quite how they were set up and used is not understood, but they could indicate the times of services, at any rate when the sun was shining. (How time was marked in small churches at other times is uncertain.) A wide variety of these 'mass' or 'scratch' dials survives and dating them is difficult; but some of them are semi-circular while others, like that from Flaunden Old Church (thirteenth-fourteenth century?), were circular (see Plate 26). They were generally about the size of a side plate and had, mounted in the centre, an indicator or 'gnomon' and a series of scratched or carved lines radiating from the midpoint. It has been suggested that the circular design might have been influenced by the appearance of clock faces (from the late thirteenth century), although, since the upper semi-circle represented night time when there was no sun, it was purely decorative or symbolic.

The Flaunden mass dial presents many puzzles. It is not even certain which way up it went. Since it was built into the wall of the church (possibly the south window, given the two worked faces) and was therefore difficult to move, it was not brought to the new church until 1949, when it was rescued by Revd T.D. Lloyd (incumbent 1939-51). The earlier markings have therefore been confused by later graffiti, some of which are probably quite recent. It is incised on a large block of stone, having a deep hole for the gnomon. The lines from there possibly extend over an earlier (and incomplete?) cross in the 'Templar' style, which marked the church's consecration (a so-called 'consecration cross'), and was formed by drawing arcs with a pair of compasses (see Plate 27). There is no indication on the dial of painting, although many dials would originally have had colouring. It is possible that it indicated the third and ninth hours after sunrise, that is the times of the morning and afternoon services – when circumstances allowed services to take place (see Chapter 2).

Plate 26. The Flaunden Mass Dial
Image courtesy of Ben Jones

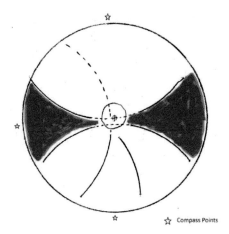

Plate 27. An incomplete consecration cross?
Diagram courtesy of Ben Jones

One item from the old church has so far gone relatively unnoticed: in the vestry of St Mary Magdalene, Latimer, there is a marble slab which can be identified as the top of the altar from Flaunden Old Church. The evidence for this is as follows.

First, the Notebook referred to above (p. 10) contains the following information about Flaunden Old Church: '(The) Commu(nio)n table, (the) top of wh(ich) is a white marble slab, is now in (the) vestry of Latimer Ch(urch)' (Plate 28).

Plate 28. Extract from the notebook in the Latimer Church Archives

Secondly, we know from Salmon (118) that 'The Chancel of Flaunden is lately beautified by Mr. Prime [Prince]; the Communion Table was given by him of grey Marble, which is wainscotted round and railed, and …'. This description fits the slab in the Latimer vestry (Plate 29).

Plate 29. Detail of the marble slab in the Latimer Vestry

Thirdly, the slab measures 61 x 100 cm, and was clearly positioned against a wall, since one of the long sides is flat whereas the others are worked. This would fit the plan proposed by Edward Blore for his work on Latimer Church in 1841, assuming that Blore's scale is in feet (Plate 30).

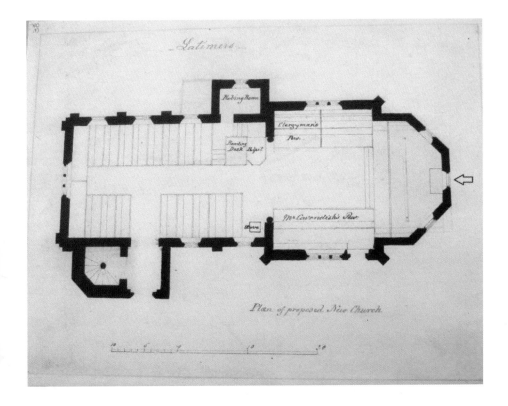

Plate 30. Blore's plan for Latimer Church (British Library Add MS 42029 f. 38)
From the British Library Collection

It seems likely that, when the new Flaunden Church was built in 1838, the altar from the old church was secured by the Revd Samuel King, Rector of both Flaunden and Latimer (1821-57), to be used in Blore's rebuilding of Latimer Church in 1841. It was then removed when the semi-circular apse of the current church was built to Sir Gilbert Scott's design in 1867, and a new altar was installed. The Revd Samuel King was, of course, Scott's uncle, for whom Scott had previously designed the 1838 Flaunden Church (see Chapter 5).

Finally, there are some false attributions. The information panel on the clock case in the new church says that the clock (Plate 31) came from the old church, but there is no sign of a clock in the surviving pictures of the church (see Plates 4, 6 and 7). According to NADFAS, quoting David Birt, Clocks Adviser to the Oxford DAC, it 'may well have come from a demolished stable block or similar'. It can be dated to the late eighteenth century, and details of its origins, maker and installation in the new church are unknown. There is no inscription in the clock itself.

Plate 31. The clock in Flaunden New Church

Sources: Cocks, Cussans, Paul Drury FSA *per litteras*, Flaunden Church Archives, *HCH* II, *IHM*, Ben Jones *per litteras*, Latimer Church Archives, NADFAS, North, Notebook, Orme, Pevsner, Stephen Rickerby *per litteras*, Rumley, Salmon, Williams

Chapter 4. Memorials

Until 1477, when Pope Sixtus IV issued a Bull (dated 7 May) empowering residents to bury their dead in the churchyard, contrary to usual practice for a chapel of ease (see Appendix 2), all burials took place at the mother church in Hemel Hempstead. There are 149 entries between 1732 and 1838 in the surviving Flaunden Burial Registers. That said, just one grave is now identifiable within the precincts of the church: the remains of the altar tomb of Richard Prince (see below), which is now almost entirely covered by rubble and vegetation. Several inscriptions are, however, reported by Cussans, 177: to Mrs Ann Godwin (died 14 July 1865), Mrs Hannah Hobbs (died 27 May 1875), James Cole (no date), Thomas Thorn (died 30 April 1870), Elizabeth Thorn (died 18 July 1872) and Mrs Sarah Busby (died 24 July 1846). All of these post-date the building of the new church up the hill (see Chapter 5), which suggests that the old church continued to be valued by some as a burial site. The churchyard is still consecrated and subject to faculty jurisdiction; the church itself is also a Grade II-listed building and is a Scheduled Monument (see Chapter 2). The results of the latest geophysical survey of the church and site are available online (see the QR code at the end of the Bibliography).

Richard Prince (buried 22 November 1743) was a significant local resident, a gentleman but from a family of yeoman stock which had lived in the area for some three hundred years, although he was the last of his line (see the tomb inscription below). For his landholdings and benefactions, both to the church and local community - he left money in his will to buy bread for the poor of both Flaunden (30 shillings) and Latimer (ten shillings) - see Chapter 3 and Appendix 3. Little is known of him otherwise.

He leaves instructions in his will (see Appendix 3) regarding his tomb. It is to be 'a proper Monument' with 'a good durable stone' placed upon it and it is to be enclosed by 'Iron Rails and palisades.' Its remains can be found in the corner made by the south of the nave and the west of the south transept (see Plate 32). Although largely obscured, the fallen railings survive (see Plates 33 and 34).

Plate 32. Drawing by H[erbert] Edmunds in 1910, showing Richard Prince's tomb
Flaunden Church Collection

Plates 33 and 34. Railings from Richard Prince's tomb

The inscription is recorded by Cussans, 178:

In Memory

of

Richard Prince Gen. of this Parish

who departed this life yᵉ 13 Nov. 1743

In yᵉ 66 Year of his Age

Also

of Jane his wife who died yᵉ 25 April

1741 Aged 67 Years.

He was a tender Husband sincere Friend

kind Master and generous Benefactor

whose Family was possessed of an Estate

In this Parish upwards of three hundred

Years which now by his Death

Is become Extinct

Cussans then describes the arms at the head of the slab.

The tomb was broken into several times in the early twentieth century by raiders apparently prompted by a local legend that Richard Prince ('former Lord of the Manor of Flaunden') had served in a number of wars and that the jewels he had brought back were buried with him: *Westminster Gazette* 24 September 1926, 7. (Alternative accounts state that the thieves were misled by the name 'Prince', which they associated with royalty.) Not surprisingly, there is no record of jewels ever having been found.

In reporting a recent tomb defilement, the special correspondent of the *Westminster Gazette* recorded, 23 September 1926, 7, that the vandals had removed a heavy lead coffin and writes: 'One half of the stone is intact, and bears the arms of some old family – presumably that of the Princes of Flaunden. I deciphered the words "Three hundred," "In Memoriam." and a date, "1461" on the stone … A broken piece of the tombstone … bears the letter in capitals, HAM,"…'. This transcription is clearly a version of that given by Cussans ('1461 misrenders 1741 and HAM is a misrendering of part of FAMILY), but the Arms he depicts (see Plate 35) agree with Cussans' description only as regards the three birds and the horizontal zigzag on the sinister (our right) side of the shield ('a Fess dancetté … between three Birds').

Plate 35 The Arms of the Prince Family?
Photographed from the Westminster Gazette, *23 September 1926*

Inside the church, set into the centre of the floor between the transepts, was a slab commemorating an earlier Richard Prince. The slab is no longer visible, and, when Cussans wrote (1879-80), was 'now mostly indecipherable' (Cussans 177). However, he prints the transcription made by the Revd Bryant Burgess in about 1870:

Here lyeth yᵉ body of
RICHARD PRINCE Late of Flanden
Yeoman who deceased yᵉ 21
day of Ianuary Anno Dom
1622 to whose Memory
his Son Ioseph did Dedicate
…………………..old Stone
And that being Decayed this
New Stone is Erected at the
Charge of RICHARD PRINCE
Son of IOHN PRINCE Gen
Ian Anno Dom 1717

As well as erecting a new stone, Richard Prince jnr gave money for raising the church floor: clear evidence that, built near the Chess, the building was liable to flooding. (For flooding, see also Chapters 1 and 5.) It is likely that this flooding was responsible for the damage to the slab in the first place and that the work on the slab and floor was done at the same time.

About two hundred yards to the east of the church, beside the footpath leading to Chenies, can be found the altar tomb of William Liberty. Although he is described in his will as 'a tilemaker in the parish of Rickmansworth in the County of Hertford' (The National Archives PROB 11/1031/119), the inscription on his tomb says he was a brickmaker, and, indeed, the tomb is built of fine brick, with a stone marker at each corner (see Plates 36 and 37). It is now surrounded by an iron railing. While the inscription is practically illegible today, it can be read on a modern plaque mounted beside the tomb (see Plates 36 and 38).

Plate 36. William Liberty's tomb

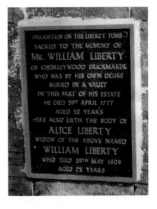

Plate 37 One of the corner markers from William Liberty's tomb

Plate 38. Inscription on William Liberty's tomb – now mounted beside the tomb
Latimer Village Box

This conflicts in minor details with the transcription (1859) of Burgess:

> Sacred to the Memory
> of Mr. William Liberty, of
> Chorley Wood, Brickmaker,
> who was by his own desire buried in
> a Vault in this part of his estate.
> He died 21 April 1777 aged 53 years.
> Here also lieth the Body of
> Mrs. Alice Liberty
> widow of the above named
> William Liberty
> She died 19 May 1809
> aged 82 years.

The tomb was erected in Liberty's orchard, outside the churchyard. There is no mention in his will of his desire to be buried here, and speculation as to his reasons has been inevitable. Foremost of these is that he was a Nonconformist, and this is certainly in keeping with the Dissenting associations of the area, conveniently documented by G. Loosley in *Buckinghamshire Examiner*, 19 March 1915, 6. (See too Chapter 2 above: the Compton Census. Compare the fear that the church might lose members to the Baptist Church, following the move of the old village up the hill: see Chapter 5.) There is also a tradition that Liberty wanted to be buried on his own estate because he feared that at time of resurrection, there would be such a scramble for bones that, if he were buried in a churchyard, he would struggle to find his.

Burgess 1859 suggests that Liberty might have derived the idea of burial on his own estate from the Grimsdell tomb on Cokes Farm, two miles distant and now in a private garden (see Plate 39).

Sources: Bastin, *Buckinghamshire Examiner*, Burgess 1859, Clutterbuck, Cussans, Farley 2000, Flaunden Church Archives, Mrs Sophie Hammond *per litteras*, Lawrence et al., Orme, Parish Registers, *Westminster Gazette*, White

Plate 39. The Grimsdell tomb

Chapter 5. Flaunden Church today

Plate 40. Flaunden New Church
Image courtesy of Andrea Norman

The site of the medieval village was gradually abandoned from about the eighteenth century, and the hamlet described by Clutterbuck in 1827, which comprised 'a few detached cottages and farm-houses' and 'maintain[ed] its own poor and appoint[ed] its own parish-officers', is presumably the new village, since the church is described as standing 'about one mile' away (Clutterbuck 139). Clutterbuck's description doubtless alludes *inter alia* to Oak Cottage and Sharlowe's Farm, late medieval hall-houses which indicate how long the new site had been occupied. Various reasons have been advanced for the abandonment of the old site, such as an outbreak of bubonic plague, but for chronological reasons, this is most unlikely. Flooding, along with the health issues raised by living in a damp valley, was probably a significant factor, however: when accused in 1764 of neglecting his duties, the chaplain, Revd Dr John Stirling, noted that the church 'stood in a very low agueish situation, and in winter stood several feet under water' (Pemberton 14). Social and economic reasons would also have been significant. The men of Flaunden old village are popularly reputed to have been 'skilled in the craft of making pikes, swords, and armour' in the 1600s (*Westminster Gazette*, 24 September 1926, 7), but no evidence has been found of industrial activity on the site. Instead, the villagers, who would originally have comprised principally the tenants of Thomas de Flaunden for whom the church was built (see Chapter 1), are likely for the most part to have remained agricultural workers, and there would never have been many of them; there was limited employment and little space in the valley for the village to expand. (The 1801 census records a population of 179, of whom 172 were chiefly employed in agriculture.) The young would naturally have moved away over time, especially to jobs in or places with easier access to towns, while the elderly would have sought the better living conditions offered by the new site.

Once the original village had been abandoned, there was pressure to build a new church on the new site: the old church was in disrepair and at some distance, especially for the elderly and for small children (it takes about 30 minutes to walk from the new village to the old church along the bridlepath and through Baldwin's wood: see Map 2). Secondly, following the construction of a Baptist Chapel in the new village in 1831 (Plate 41) and the formation of a Baptist church in 1836, there was perhaps a fear that congregation members would be lost to them; and, in any case, the old church was very small (see Chapter 2 and Plate 45).

Plate 41. The old Baptist Chapel in Flaunden

The decision was therefore made, by the Reverend Samuel King, to build a new church at the west end of the village (see Appendix 4). (Mr King, for whom see Plate 43, was incumbent of Latimer and Flaunden, although the two churches were not officially united as a single benefice in the Diocese of Oxford until 1876.) The church was designed by a youthful George Gilbert Scott, King's nephew by marriage, who had lived in Latimer for a year as a teenager, who knew and had sketched the old church, and had received a good deal of encouragement and early architectural training from King (Plate 44). It was completed in 1838, funded by private subscription and a grant from the Incorporated Society for the enlargement, building and repairing of Churches and Chapels (see Appendix 4 and Plate 45). Scott is very dismissive of the church, which is pre-Gothic Revival, describing it in his memoirs as 'the poor barn designed for my uncle King' (Scott 86). Compare Plate 42, a note from Lady Susan Trueman, granddaughter (through her mother) of the first Lord Chesham, saying that he was so ashamed of it that he wanted to rebuild it. This shame is hardly justified, however. (Plate 40).

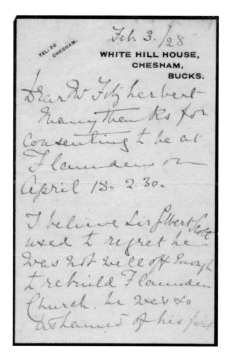
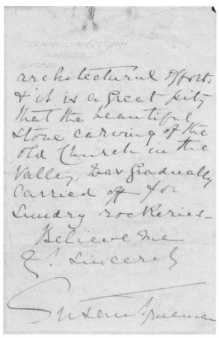

Plate 42. Note from Lady Susan Trueman *to Revd H.E. Fitzherbert (Incumbent 1927-30)* about Gilbert Scott and Flaunden New Church

Flaunden Church Archives

Plate 43. The Revd Samuel King
Photographed from Reverend Samuel King -
gilbertscott.org

Plate 44. Sir Gilbert Scott 1879, by Anna
Lea Merritt, after George Richmond
© 2023 Dean and Chapter of Westminster

The foundation inscription of the new church, as recorded in what became the *Hertford Mercury and Reformer*, 29 August 1837, 2, reads as follows:

> *The Stone in which this Writing is inclosed was laid August 12ᵗʰ, A.D. 1837, in the First Year of the Reign of our Sovereign Lady Queen VICTORIA, by the Lady Catherine Cavendish, of Latimer, in the adjoining County of Buckingham, and Parish of Chesham – the Old Church of Flaunden being in a RUINOUS state, and situate two miles south of this spot, on the banks of the river. This New Church is building by Private Subscription, closely adjoining the Village, for the convenience of the Inhabitants, and with the desire of promoting their Spiritual Benefit, and of advancing the Glory of Almighty God. The Right Rev. John Kaye, DD, Bishop of Lincoln, Diocesan, the Honourable Charles Compton Cavendish, M.P., patron; the Rev. Samuel King, M.A., Rector of Latimer, incumbent; the Rev. Francis George Jackson, B.A. curate*

Alas, the position of this foundation stone is unknown.

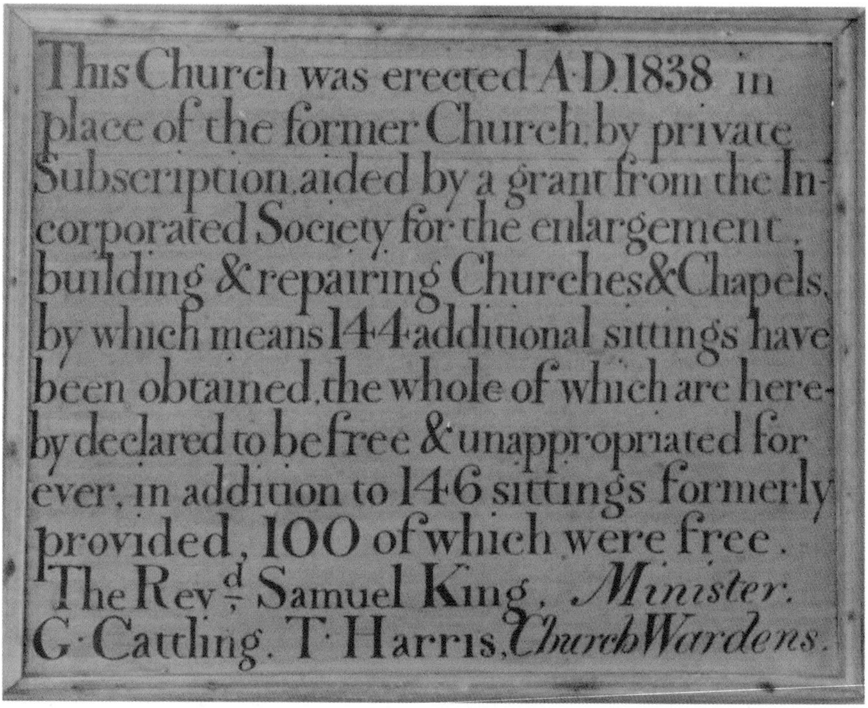

Plate 45. Dedication Board in Flaunden New Church

Sources: Branigan 1968, *Buckinghamshire Examiner*, Burgess 1859, Clutterbuck, Flaunden Church Archives, Hawkes, *HCH* II, *Hertford Mercury and Reformer*, Lawrence et al., *London Gazette*, Parish Registers, Pevsner, Rees, Scott, *Westminster Gazette*

Appendix 1. Photographs of Flaunden Old Church

now in the Hertfordshire Archives, from the collection of Andrew Whitford Anderson (1859-1950), a Watford architect.

Description	Date	Catalogue No.
N. transept with remains of wall painting	30 August 1894	DE/X1042/8/13a
View of ruins of the church from the SE	30 August 1894	DE/X1042/8/13b
W. doorway from outside (see Plate 8)	7 April 1906	DE/X1042/8/14a
Interior, looking W.	7 April 1906	DE/X1042/8/14b
Interior, S. transept window	7 April 1906	DE/X1042/8/14c
Interior, S. transept showing reredos	7 April 1906	DE/X1042/8/15a
N. transept window showing wall painting (see Plate 10)	7 April 1906	DE/X1042/8/15b
Tiles from old church in porch of new church	1916	DE/X1042/8/15c
W. doorway from outside	24 April 1922	DE/X1042/8/16a
Interior, looking W.	24 April 1922	DE/X1042/8/16b
Interior, S. transept, showing piscina	24 April 1922	DE/X1042/8/17

Appendix 2. Bull of Pope Sixtus IV regarding burials at Flaunden Old Church

Ex Archivis Ecc: Lincoln Reg: Rotherham. fo. 121: Lincolnshire Archives DIOC/REG/21, as transcribed by Clutterbuck, 139

Note on the translation: the Latin is late, at times ungrammatical and obscure, supplementary words and explanations need occasionally to be added for clarity, and the document is formulaic in character and therefore occasionally verbose. Its general import is nonetheless clear.

Sixtus Episcopus servus servorum Dei, &c. Exhibita nobis pro parte dilectorum filiorum parochialis capellae Sanctae Mariae Magdalenae de Flaunden, Lincolniensis dioceseos, petitio continebat, quod licet ad dictam capellam, quae parochialis ecclesiae de Hemel Hempsted dictae dioceseos filialis existit, parochiani predicti pro sacris ecclesiae, praeterquam sepulturam accedere consueverunt; ipsorum tamen parochianorum decedentium corpora nec in capella nec ecclesia hujusmodi, ex eo quod ab illa per quinque milliaria distant, a tanto tempore cujus hominum memoria in contrarium non existit, visa sunt sepeliri, nec indies sepeliuntur; et si ad praedictam ecclesiam corpora parochianorum hujusmodi pro illorum sepultura deferuntur, propter inundationem aquarum quam in partibus illis, et maxime tempore hyemis, sepe eveniunt, personis ipsa corpora deferentibus pericula multa evenire possent; quare, pro parte dictorum parochianorum, nobis fuit humiliter supplicatum, ut, in ipsa capella, moderno et pro tempore divinis deservienti capellano, ut ipsorum parochianorum pro tempore decedentium corpora in capella seu illius cimeterio perpetuo sepeliri facere possit, concedere et indulgere, aliaque quae in premissis oporteat providere, de benignitate apostolica, dignaremur: nos hujusmodi supplicationibus inclinati, moderno et pro tempore in eadem capella deservienti capellano, ut ipsorum parochianorum decedentium corpora in capella seu illius cimiterio hujusmodi perpetuo sepeliri facere possit, constitutionibus et ordinationibus apostolicis bonae memoriae Octonis et Octoboni olim in regno Angliae apostolicae sedis legatorum, ac in procurationibus et synodalibus concilio editis generali, constitutionibus et ordinationibus ceterisque contrariis nequaquam obstantibus, auctoritate apostolica seu tenore praesentium, concedimus et indulgemus, jure parochialis ecclesiae, et cujuslibet alterius in omnibus semper salvo. Nulli ergo hominum liceat, &c. Datum Romae apud Sanctum Petrum, anno millesimo quadringentesimo septuagesimo septimo, septimo Maii, et pontificatus nostri sexto.

Sixtus, bishop, servant of the servants of God, etc. [i.e. to the addressee]. A petition shown to us on behalf of our beloved sons of the parochial chapel of St Mary Magdalene of Flaunden in the diocese of Lincoln stated that though the aforesaid parishioners have been accustomed to go to the said chapel, which is a dependent of the parish church of Hemel Hempstead in the said diocese, for the services of the church with the exception of burial, yet the bodies of those same parishioners when deceased seem not to have been buried within living memory or customarily nowadays either in the chapel or in a church of this kind, because they are five miles away from it [i.e. the parish church]; and if the bodies of such parishioners are carried to the aforesaid church for burial, many dangers could arise for the persons carrying the bodies, because of the floods which [reading *quae*] often happen in those parts, and especially in winter-time. Therefore, humble supplication was made to us, on behalf of the said parishioners, that we grant our favour and assent to the present chaplain conducting divine service in that chapel for the time being that he can have the bodies of the parishioners as they die buried in the chapel or in its cemetery for evermore, and that we might, in our apostolic good will, <assent> to other things which ought to be seen to in what has been set out above. Swayed by supplications to this effect, by apostolic authority and the purport of the present document we concede and grant to the present chaplain conducting divine service in the same chapel for the time being that he may have the bodies of parishioners when they die buried for all time in the chapel or in its cemetery of this kind, according to the decrees and apostolic ordinances of Otto and Ottobonus of blessed memory, at one time legates of the apostolic see in the kingdom of England [Otto of Tonenga, legate 1225-6, and Ottobuono Fieschi, later Pope Adrian V, legate 1265 to 1268] and in the procurations [i.e. provisions] and synodal decrees issued in general council, the constitutions and ordinances and diverse other things notwithstanding, always saving the rights of the parish church and any other in all things. Therefore let it be permitted to no man etc. [i.e. to contest or act contrary to the above decision]. Given in Rome, at St Peter's, in the year 1477, on 7th May, in the sixth year of our pontificate.

Appendix 3. Extracts from the will of Richard Prince
The National Archives PROB 11/730/430

In the Name of God Amen I *Richard Prince of Flanden in the County of Hertford Gentleman being mindfull of my Mortality do make and ordain this my Last Will and Testament in writing concerning my Real and personal Estate in manner and form following that is to say ... I give and bequeath unto my Nephew Prince Child of all and every my Household Goods Goods [sic] Chattels Cattle Stock Implements of Husbandry Ready moneys Mortgages Bonds and Securitys for moneys ... I order and direct my Executors to pay ... to the poor of Flanden aforesaid the sum of thirty shillings which my will and mind is shall be laid out in bread and distributed to and amongst the poor of Flanden aforesaid and unto the poor of Lattimers Hamlett in the parish of Chesham aforesaid the sum of ten shillings to be laid out in Bread and distributed unto and amongst the poor of the said Hamlett only ... And moreover I give and devise unto my said Nephew Prince Child all those Peices or Parcells of land lying near to and in the Parish of Chesham aforesaid called Spratts Hills [off what is now Fullers Hill, to the SW of Chesham, SP 955 010] with their Appurtenances To hold to him his Heirs and Assigns for ever In Trust that he or they do and shall erect and build a proper Monument for me and thereon put and place a good durable stone and inclose the same with Iron Rails and palisades ... And Lastly I do hereby revoke and make void all former and other Wills and Codicils by me before made In Witness whereof I the said Richard Prince have set to this my last Will and Testament contained in four sheets of Paper set my hand to the bottom of the three first sheets thereof and my hand and Seal to the fourth and last sheet thereof this four and twentyeth day of September in the year of our Lord one thousand seven hundred and forty two [signed]* Ri(char)d Prince *Signed Sealed Published and declared by the said Richard Prince the Testator as and for his last Will and Testament in the presence of us ... as Witnesses thereto ... [signed]* Henry Woodbridge Francis Shrimpton *[ut vid.]* John Wade

Appendix 4. Petition submitted for the Consecration of Flaunden New Church
Lincolnshire Archives DIOC/CONSEC BUNDLE/271/4

To the Right Reverend Father in God John by Divine permission Lord Bishop of Lincoln The humble Petition of the Reverend Samuel King Perpetual Curate of the Perpetual Curacy and Parish church of Flaunden in the County of Hertford and Diocese of Lincoln. And of George Catling and Thomas Harris Churchwardens of the said Parish, and of the undersigned Inhabitants thereof Sheweth That the Parish Church of Flaunden aforesaid being in a decayed and ruinous state and very inconveniently situated for the Parishioners of the said Parish being nearly two miles distant from their Dwelling houses it was deemed adviseable to take down the same and build a new Church in a more convenient situation within the said Parish – That William Grover of Wendover Dean in the county of Buckingham Esquire hath voluntarily given a piece of Copyhold Land situate in Flaunden aforesaid and near to the Dwelling houses of the Parishioners and Inhabitants containing by admeasurement Seventy two poles. Which has since been enfranchised and duly conveyed to Her Majesty's Commissioners for building new Churches, to be devoted when consecrated to Ecclesiastical purposes for ever. – That your Petitioners have accordingly taken down the said church and with the assistance of other Persons of the Church of England aided by a Grant of the Sum of One hundred and Seventy pounds from the Incorporated Society for enlarging and rebuilding churches and Chapels have on part of the said piece of Land erected and built a new church containing in length fifty three feet and in width twenty two feet and fitted it up with Pews and Seats for the reception of the Parishioners and Inhabitants of the said Parish of Flaunden and furnished it with all things necessary for the performance of Divine Worship, and it is now in all respects fit and ready for Consecration And that the position of the said piece of Land not occupied by the said Church is intended for a Burial Ground and has been properly inclosed and is now in all respects fit and ready for consecration Your Petitioners therefore humbly pray that your Lordship will be pleased to consecrate the said church, and dedicate the same to the Service of Almighty God and the celebration of Divine Service according to the Rites and Ceremonies of the united Church of England and Ireland by the name of Saint Mary Magdalene And that you will further be pleased to consecrate the said remaining piece of Land as and for a Burial Ground for the use of the Parishioners and Inhabitants of the said Parish. – And Your Petitioners will ever pray etc.

[Dated June 1838 and signed by Revd Samuel King, the two Churchwardens (the illiterate Thomas Harris signed with an *X*) and five parishioners/inhabitants of the Parish: George Dodd, Henry Childs, William Harris, Robert Sexton and Joseph Abbee.]

Bibliography and Abbreviations

1898 OS map: View map: Ordnance Survey, Buckinghamshire XLIII.3 (Amersham; Chenies; Flaunden; Latimer) – Ordnance Survey 25 inch England and Wales, 1841-1952 (nls.uk), accessed February 2024

Bastin: George Bastin, 'The Hertfordshire village that stole away', *Hertfordshire Countryside* 51 no. 205 (1976), 26-7

Beresford: M.W. Beresford, J.G. Hurst, J. Sheail, The Deserted Medieval Village Research Group, 13th Annual Report 1965 (see archiveDownload (archaeologydataservice.ac.uk), accessed February 2024)

Branigan 1968: Keith Branigan, 'The Deserted Village of Flaunden', *Rickmansworth Historian* 16 (1968), 400-2

Branigan 1971: Keith Branigan, *Latimer, Roman, Dark Age and Early Modern Farm* (Chess Valley Archaeological and Historical Society), Bristol 1971

British Listed Buildings: Ruins of Old Church of St Mary Magdalen (650 Metres to West of Mill Farm), Chenies, Buckinghamshire (britishlistedbuildings.co.uk), accessed February 2024)

Buckinghamshire Examiner, Chesham/Uxbridge 1906-2019

Burgess 1859: Bryant Burgess, letter in *Records of Buckinghamshire* Vol. II, Aylesbury 1863, pp. 148-50 (see Records of Buckinghamshire, Or, Papers and Notes on the History, Antiquities ... : Buckinghamshire Archaeological Society: Free Download, Borrow, and Streaming: Internet Archive, accessed February 2024)

Burgess 1887: Bryant Burgess, 'Latimers or Latimer', *Records of Buckinghamshire* 6 (1887), 28-47 (see rob_6_1_27.pdf (bucksas.org.uk), accessed February 2024)

Cauvain: Pauline and Stanley Cauvain, 'New discoveries of Penn tiles', *Records of Buckinghamshire* 33 (1991), 44-8 (see rob_33_0_44.pdf (bucksas.org.uk), accessed February 2024)

Chauncy: Henry Chauncy, *The Historical Antiquities of Hertfordshire*, London 1826 (see The historical antiquities of Hertfordshire - sir Henry Chauncy - Google Books, accessed February 2024)

Clutterbuck: Robert Clutterbuck, *The History and Antiquities of the County of Hertford* Vol. III, London 1827

Cocks: A.H. Cocks, *The Church Bells of Buckinghamshire. Their Inscriptions, Founders, Uses, and Traditions*, London 1897 (see https://archive.org/details/cu31924011346453/mode/2up?ref=ol&view=theate, accessed February 2024)

Cussans: John Edwin Cussans, *History of Hertfordshire Vol. III containing the History of the Hundreds of Dacorum and Cashio*, London 1881 (see History of Hertfordshire - John Edwin Cussans - Google Books, accessed February 2024)

Eames, Elizabeth, *Medieval Craftsmen. English Tilers*, London 1992, reprinted 2000

Ekwall: Eilert Ekwall ed., *The Concise Oxford Dictionary of English Placenames*, 4th ed., Oxford 1960

Farley 2000: Michael Farley, *Watching Brief at the site of St Mary Magdalene Church, Flaunden, Buckinghamshire*, Michael Farley Archaeology 2000 (see Farley Watching Brief.pdf, accessed February 2024)

Farley 2010: Michael Farley ed., *An Illustrated History of Early Buckinghamshire*, Aylesbury 2010

Green, Miles, *Medieval Penn Floor Tiles*, privately published 2003

Hawkes: Peter Hawkes, 'The ruined church by the River Chess', *Chesham Town Talk* 1996, 5 (see The story of Flaunden old church - Chesham Heritage | Facebook, accessed February 2024)

HCH II: William Page, *A History of the County of Hertford: Volume 2*, London, 1908 (see *British History Online* http://www.british-history.ac.uk/vch/herts/vol2/pp215-230, accessed February 2024)

Heritage Portal: https://heritageportal.buckinghamshire.gov.uk/Monument/MBC14877, accessed February 2024)

Hertford Mercury and Reformer, established as *The Reformer*, Hertford 1834

Hohler: Christopher Hohler, 'Medieval Pavingtiles in Buckinghamshire', *Records of Buckinghamshire* 14.1 (1940-1), 1-49 and 14.2 (1942), 99-132 (see rob_14_1_1.pdf (bucksas.org.uk) and rob_14_2_99.pdf (bucksas.org.uk), accessed February 2024)

IHM: An Inventory of the Historical Monuments in Hertfordshire, London, 1910 (see *British History Online* http://www.british-history.ac.uk/rchme/herts/pp89-90, accessed February 2024)

Lawrence et al.: Margaret Lawrence, Jill Saunders, Louise Thompson, Mary Willans, *Flaunden. The Past, Present & Future*, Flaunden n.d. (but produced to accompany millennium celebrations in 2000)

Leach: Leach, Robin, *St Mary Magdalene Church and Flaunden Village*, June 1994 and August 2012, updating Macgregor [Page references are to the 1994 edition; the 2012 edition is without page numbers]

Leary: T.J. Leary, *A Church by the Chess. St Mary Magdalene, Latimer*, Chesham 2023

LiDAR: Beacons of the Past LiDAR Portal (see Courses - Beacons of the Past LiDAR Portal (chilternsbeacons.org), accessed March 2024)

London Gazette, 4 April 1876, 2280

Macgregor: Macgregor, Andrew M, *Flaunden. A celebration of the 150th anniversary of St Mary Magdalene Church 1838-1988*, Flaunden June 1988

Mawer: Allen Mawer ed., *The Chief Elements used in English Place-Names*, Cambridge 1924

NADFAS: *St Mary Magdalene, Flaunden, Hertfordshire, Record of Church Furnishings*, The National Association of Decorative and Fine Arts Societies (now the Church Recording Society), n.d. (but recording carried out in 2005-6)

North: Thomas North and J.C.L. Stahlschmidt, *The Church Bells of Hertfordshire. Their founders, inscriptions, traditions and peculiar uses*, London 1886 (see The Church Bells of Hertfordshire - Google Books, accessed February 2024)

Notebook: It is not known who kept this notebook (in the Latimer Church Archives), but it has stamped on the cover 'Latimer Rectory, Chesham, Bucks' and is inscribed 'Please return to ~~Rev. H.E. Fitzherbert~~ T.D. Lloyd Rector.' Fitzherbert was Rector 1927-30 and Lloyd was Rector 1939-51. Fitzherbert's handwriting on the front of the book is not that of the notebook's compiler, although it is the same as some of the pencilled marginalia.

Orme: Nicholas Orme, 'Church and Chapel in Medieval England', *Transactions of the Royal Historical Society* 6 (1996), 75-102

Parish Registers: Parish Registers. Latimer & Flaunden. DVD C554. Buckinghamshire Family History Society

Pemberton: W.A. Pemberton, 'Bovingdon and Flaunden, 1746. A negligent minister in trouble', *Hertfordshire Past* 16 (1984), 6-19

Pevsner: Nikolaus Pevsner, second edition revised Nicholas Pevsner and Bridget Cherry 1977, third edition revised James Bettley, *The Buildings of England. Hertfordshire*, New Haven and London 2019

Rees: Neil Rees, 'The local legacy of the famous architect George Gilbert Scott' (see <u>The local legacy of the famous architect George Gilbert Scott - Chesham Museum)</u>, accessed February 2024)

Rumley: Peter T.J. Rumley, 'Medieval Mass Dials Decoded', <u>www.buildingconservation.com</u>, accessed February 2024

Salmon: Nathanael Salmon, *The history of Hertfordshire; describing the county and its antient monuments, particularly the Roman*, London 1728 (see <u>The history of Hertfordshire; describing the county and its antient monuments, particularly the Roman: Salmon, N. (Nathanael), 1675-1742: Free Download, Borrow, and Streaming: Internet Archive</u>, accessed February 2024)

Scott: Sir George Gilbert Scott, *Personal and Professional Recollections*, ed. G. Gilbert Scott, London 1879 (see <u>Personal and professional recollections: Scott, George Gilbert, Sir, 1811-1878: Free Download, Borrow, and Streaming: Internet Archive</u>, accessed February 2024)

SPAB: 'Old Flaunden Church'. Report by the Secretary of the Society for the Protection of Ancient Buildings, April 1928 (Flaunden Church Archives)

Van Lemmen: Hans Van Lemmen, *Medieval Tiles*, Oxford and New York 2000

Westminster Gazette, London 1893-1928

White: Ivor White, *A History of Little Chalfont*, Little Chalfont 1993

Whiteman: Anne Whiteman and Mary Clapinson, *The Compton Census of 1676. A Critical Edition*, London 1986

Williams, Chris H.K. Williams, 'The Evolution of English Mass & Scratch Dials c. 1250 – c. 1650', Part 1 – Dial Categorisation, *British Sundial Society Bulletin* 22 (2010), 24-6; Part 2 – Dials by Type Categorisation, ibid. 42-4

For updates on archaeological investigations of the site, scan the QR code, which will take you to the Chilterns Heritage and Archaeology Partnership homepage. Look for the links to 'Flaunden'.

Index of Names

Abbee, Joseph 38
Anderson, Andrew Whitford 35

Bingham, Revd William 8
Birt, David 22
Blore, Edward vi, 21
Buckler, J. 5-6, 15
Burgess, Revd Bryant 26, 28, 34
Busby, Mrs Sarah 23

Catling, George 38
Cavendish, Charles Compton (first Lord Chesham, 1858-63) 9, 32-3
Cavendish, Lady Catherine, (first Lady Chesham) 33
Cavendish, William George, (second Lord Chesham, 1863-82) 9
Chesham: see Cavendish
Childs, Henry 38
Cole, James 23
Cooke, W.B. iv, 4

de Flaunden, Nicholas 2
de Flaunden, Thomas 3, 31
de Graveleigh, Bernardus 3
Dodd, George 38

Edmunds, Herbert vi, 5, 24
Edward VI, King 10
Elizabeth I, Queen 14

Fitzherbert, Revd H.E. viii, 32, 40-1

Godwin, Mrs Ann 23
Grimsdell family vi, 28-9
Grover, William 38

Harris, Thomas 38
Harris, William 38
Hobbs, Mrs Hannah 23

Hohler, Christopher 16-17

Jackson. Revd Francis George 33

Kaye, the Right Revd Dr John 33, 38
King, Revd Samuel vi, 21, 32-3, 38
Knight, William vi, 12-13

Liberty, Mrs Alice 28
Liberty, William vi, 27-8
Lloyd, Revd T.D. 19, 40-1
Loosley, G. 28

Mary, mother of Christ 10
Merritt, Anna Lee 33
Munro, Henry iv, vi, 4

Otto of Tonenga 36
Ottobuono Fieschi 36

Pope Adrian V (see Ottobuono Fieschi)
Pope Sixtus IV 23, 35-6
Prince Child (nephew of Richard Prince jnr, q.v.) 37
Prince family vi-vii, 12, 25-6
Prince, Jane (wife of Richard Prince jnr, q.v.) 25
Prince, John (father of Richard Prince jnr, q.v.) 26
Prince, Joseph (son of Richard Prince snr, q.v.) 26
Prince, Richard jnr v-vi, 14-15, 20, 23-7, 37
Prince, Richard snr 26

St Mary Magdalene vi, 1, 8, 38
Saxton, Christopher 3
Scott, George Gilbert vi, 21, 32-3
Sexton, Robert 38
Shrimpton, Francis 37

Stirling, Revd Dr John 30

Thorn, Elizabeth 23
Thorn, Thomas 23
Trueman, Lady Susan vi, 32

Victoria, Queen 33

Wade, John 37
Woodbridge, Henry 37

General Index

Altar 10, 20-1; altar cloth 10

Archaeology 1, 3, 23, 41. See also 'Flaunden Old Church site', 'LiDAR'

Architecture vii-viii, 4, 10, 21, 32, 35; Gothic revival 32; Greek cross 4. See also 'Hertfordshire spike', 'Plan'

Baldwin's Wood 31

Beacon Hill 17

Bells vi, 5, 9-13; clapper vi, 13; handbells 10-11; Whitechapel Foundry 13

Benefaction vi-vii, 12, 14-15, 20, 23, 25, 26-7, 30, 37

Berkhamsted, Deanery of 3

Bovingdon 3, 8-9

Buckinghamshire 33, 38

Candles and candlestick 10

Catholicism 10, 12, 14

Cemetery vii, 23, 28, 35-6, 38

Censer 10

Census 1801: 31; Compton census 4, 28

Chancel: Plan (inside front cover), 4-5, 7, 10-11, 20

Chenies 1, 27

Chenies Manor vii, 14

Chesham 1, 2, 37; Parish of 33, 37. See also 'Fullers Hill', 'Spratts Hill'

Chess Valley v-vii, 1-3, 30-1; Chess Valley Walk viii, 1. See also 'Chess, River'

Chess, River vii, 1-3, 27, 33. See also 'Flooding', 'Water supply'

Chorleywood ix, 28

Churches *passim*; Bovingdon 3, 8-9; Buntingford 4, chapel of ease 3, 15, 23; Flaunden Baptist Chapel/Church vi, 28, 31; Church of England (and Ireland) 38; Flaunden Old Church *passim*, and see also 'Flaunden Old Church site'; Flaunden New Church v-viii, 7, 10-13, 16, 19, 21-3, 30-5, 38; Great Gaddesden 8; St Mary's, Hemel Hempstead 3, 8, 23, 35-6; St Mary Magdalene, Latimer vi, viii-ix, 10, 20-1, 32-3; Letchworth 4; Sarratt 4; St John's, Uxbridge Moor vi, 12; St Peter's, Rome 36-7; Quebec Chapel 9

Clerical neglect 8-9, 30. See also 'Services'

Clocks vi, 13, 19, 21-2

Cokes Farm 28

Communion rail vi, 18

Consecration v, 19, 38; Consecration cross v, 19, 20

Cross 10-11; Templar cross 19. See also 'Architecture: Greek cross', 'Consecration: Consecration cross', 'Inscription: Maltese cross'

Diocese 14; of Lincoln 3, 8, 35-6, 38; Oxford 32

Dissolution of the Monasteries 10

Domesday Book 2

Doors and doorways vi, 4-5, 7, 18, 35

Economic activity 30-1

Edwardian inventory 5, 8, 10-14

England 10, 36

Faculty jurisdiction 23

Flaunden Old Church site iv, vii-ix, 1-2, 23, 30-1. See also 'Scheduled monument', 'Archaeology', 'Faculty jurisdiction', Listed building'

Flaunden *passim*; medieval village vii, 1-4, 28, 30-1; new village vi-vii, 3, 30-3; manor of 2, 25; name 2; parish of 9, 14, 25, 30, 35-8. See also 'Chess Valley', 'Churches', 'Economic Activity', 'Flooding', 'Oak Cottage', 'Public health', 'Sharlowes Farm', 'Water supply'

Flooding 2, 27, 30, 36

Floor 18, 26-7

Font vi, 15

Fullers Hill 37

Graffiti 19

Grave vi, 23-9, 37

Hemel Hempstead vii, 2-3,9, 35-6; Manor of 2; Vicar of 3, 8. See also 'Churches'

Heraldry vi, 25-6

Hertfordshire 3-4, 27, 37-8

Hertfordshire spike 5

Incorporated Society for the enlargement, building and repairing of Churches and Chapels 32, 38

Inscription vi, 12-14, 22-3, 25-7, 28, 33; Maltese cross 12

Latimer vii-viii, 1, 3, 9, 21-3, 27, 32-3, 37; Latimer Park Farm vi, 1, 2. See also 'Churches'

Latin 12, 35

LiDAR 1

Lincoln: see 'Diocese'

Listed building 23

Mass dial vi, 19

Metal 2, 10, 12-15, 18, 23, 25, 27, 37

Middle Ages vi-vii, 1-2, 15, 17-19, 30

Nave: Plan (inside front cover), 4, 7, 23

Niche 7, 10

Non conformists 4, 8, 28, 31. See also 'Churches'

Oak Cottage 30

Oxford: see 'Diocese'

Papal bull v, 15, 23, 35-6

Parish registers 9, 23

Parishioners and local inhabitants vii-viii, 2, 5, 9, 23, 30, 33, 35-8

Penn 17, 18

Piscina 7, 10

Plan: inside front cover

Plate: chalice vi, 13-14; paten vi, 14; salver vi, 14-15

Porch 16-18, 35

Pottery 3. See also 'Tiles'

Priest's accommodation vi, 5

Protestantism 4, 14. See also 'Non conformists'

Public health 30-1

Reading 12

Reformation 12, 14. See also 'Dissolution of the Monasteries'

Reredos 7, 10

Rickmansworth, Parish of 27

Romans 1

Roof 7, 9

Sarratt 1, 4

Saxons 2

Scheduled monument 4, 23

Scratch dial: see 'Mass dial'

Services vi-vii, 8-9, 15, 19, 35-6, 38; burial 8, 15, 35-6; communion 14; consecration v, 19, 38; Patronal service 1928: 7-8

Sharlowe's Farm 30

Spratts Hill 37

Stone: chalk 1; clunch 5; flint 1, 5; limestone 5; marble vi, 20-1; pudding-stone 5; rubble viii, 5, 23

Sundial: see 'Mass dial'

Tiles vi, 16-18, 35; tile manufacture 16-18, 27

Tower 5, 9, 11

Tradition 9, 14, 28

Transepts 4, 7, 26; north: Plan (inside front cover), vi, 5, 10-11, 35; south: Plan (inside front cover), 5, 7, 8 10, 23, 35

Vandalism viii, 25. See also 'Graffiti'

Vestments 8, 10

Victorian 18

Wall paintings vi, 10-11, 35

Walls 5, 7, 9-11, 19, 21

Water supply vi, 1-3

Watford 35

Wendover Dean 38

Will v, 23, 27-8, 37

Windows 5, 10-11, 19, 35

Wood 5, 10, 13, 18

Woodland 1, 2